NEW SONGS FOR ORPHEUS

THE HUGH MacLENNAN POETRY SERIES

Editors: Allan Hepburn and Carolyn Smart

Recent titles in the series

New Songs
for Orpheus

JOHN REIBETANZ

McGill-Queen's University Press
Montreal & Kingston • London • Chicago

ISBN 978-0-2280-1694-6 (paper)
ISBN 978-0-2280-1740-0 (ePDF)
ISBN 978-0-2280-1741-7 (ePUB)

Legal deposit second quarter 2023
Bibliothèque nationale du Québec

Printed in Canada on acid-free paper that is 100% ancient forest free
(100% post-consumer recycled), processed chlorine free

| Funded by the Government of Canada | Financé par le gouvernement du Canada |  | Conseil des arts du Canada | Canada Council for the Arts |

We acknowledge the support of the Canada Council for the Arts.

Nous remercions le Conseil des arts du Canada de son soutien.

Library and Archives Canada Cataloguing in Publication

Title: New songs for orpheus / John Reibetanz.

Names: Reibetanz, John, 1944- author.

Series: Hugh MacLennan poetry series.

Description: Series statement: The Hugh MacLennan poetry series

Identifiers: Canadiana (print) 20220452644 | Canadiana
(ebook) 20220452679 | ISBN 9780228016946 (softcover) |
ISBN 9780228017417 (ePUB) | ISBN 9780228017400 (ePDF)

Classification: LCC PS8585.E448 N49 2023 | DDC C811/.54—dc23

This book was typeset by Marquis Interscript in 9.5/13 Sabon.

In Memory of J.M.R.
and our harmonies

CONTENTS

Contents

Contents

VII. The Chorus

"Words, vowels and phonemes are so many ways of 'singing' the world."

Maurice Merleau-Ponty, *Phenomenology of Perception*

"'Singing the world' can just as well refer to the color patterns of the Caribbean reef squid, the gestures of lizards, and the scents in the trails of ants."

Eva Meijers, *When Animals Speak*

I

The Music

THEIR SONG

With such songs the bard of Thrace
drew the trees, held beasts enthralled
and constrained stones to follow him.
                    Ovid, *Metamorphoses* XI, 1–2

For a change Orpheus
listens to the other
musicians once the hum
of his lyre no longer
hangs like moss from branches
in the forest air
or in his ear's arched groves

first he catches only
louder instruments as
lungs bellow loss
echoing letdown of milk
for departed calves
or a lamb's vibrato laments
the passing of its sole spring

then he makes out frogs'
miniature bagpipes
guzzling air before
the dive beneath it
to their long cold
silent sostenuto
in the pond's underworld

by nightfall his ears pick up
the bell-like notes of bats
tolling their exile from light
and the staccato scream
of breath through the reed flute
of a death's-head moth
tattooed with grief from birth

as each voice cries its lost
Eurydice the marriage
of flesh and soul that ends
too soon too soon Orpheus
picks up his lyre again
and sings the song of breath
which is theirs and his

THE DRUM

She merely returns the words she hears ...
for voice, and voice alone, still lives in her.
                    Ovid, *Metamorphoses* III, 368–9, 400

   We're all brothers and sisters
of Echo returning the words
   we hear those words that floated
in air before we came onstage
   and after our curtain call
will be a newer voice's script
   passing the tongue's borrowed songs
from one body to another

   each touched by a sensation
that unlike light does not stop short
   at a glass threshold of flesh
but enters your ear's arched doorway
   caresses the skin's fine hair
beats a small drum to gain access
   to circuits that turn your mind's
receiver on and in return

   your throat releases the sounds
that your tongue shapes to summon up
   a world transformed like Echo
into living voice and knocking
   at the doors of other ears
not limiting the range of its
   let's say to a bounded is
but letting it expand as in

let's say Echo is a child
whose voice calls up blue seas from the
   green sea around the sandbox
her words transform into a ship
   and when the years transform her
into an adult – *let's say* a
   marine biologist who
has learned to know the deeps by ear –

   she hypothesizes that
the songs of humpback whales are not
   mere sound but voice and follows
their echo patterns far beyond
   the range of human hearing
deciphering the whale language
   as the drum of her *let's say*
transforms *perhaps* to boundless *is*

MINSTRELS

If only she could speak, she would tell her name
and sad misfortune, and beg for aid. But instead ...
she did tell the sad story of her changed form
with letters which she traced in the dust with her hoof.
                          Ovid, *Metamorphoses* I, 647–50

The air and the waters are filled
with sad and happy ballads that
float free of words and letters tales
of captivity groaned out by
the beetle pent up in a child's
small hand or sea shanties piped at
minnow family reunions.

Unlike Io fledglings can beg
for aid from parent wrens who keep
in touch through their companion cries
while in a log beneath their nest
bess-bug larvae susurrations
answer the interrogations
rapped out by six-legged relations.

On remote islands guillemots
sing over their flocks' wall of sound
to weave colourful madrigals
for their own particular brood
who recognize the voiceprint at
music hour and come scuttling home
to the correct cleft in the cliff.

Around those islands humpback whales
politely call one another
by the proper names (each unique
to its maritime addressee)
that baffled Io's bovine tongue
before they embark on yarns with
musical ornamentation.

To be so cowed by animal
lyrics Io must never have
fully been a cow endowed with
all a cow's lowing resources
and must have felt relieved returned
to an isle of words safe harboured
from the sea of other singers.

Through those lips, to which rocks listened,
and to which the hearts of savage
beasts responded, the soul, breathed out,
went faring forth.

Ovid, *Metamorphoses* XI, 41–3

We can never know whether
rock listened to chanting voices
　　while lips were blowing pigment
onto cave walls into which sound
　　vanished forever unlike
the red ochre that has embraced
　　rock for thirty thousand years
singing animal songs to it

　　some about creatures that have
no other life except in song
　　aurochs and woolly mammoth
whose weaponed heads did not save them
　　from dying out like echoes
others who lingered long enough
　　to enter another life
in the cave of the human mind

where lions offer our dreams
fleetness and daring and where deer
freezing give shape to our fears
in an installation of words
more portable than frescoes ·
lips breathing out sounds that summon
ghostly after-images
of breathers beyond the cave mouth

some now far beneath the earth
among tree roots' long winding caves
which image the underworld
of language its indirections
intersections gnarled unex-
pected rhythmical turns if you
listen closely you will hear
the breathed-out souls lingering there

II

Wings of Song

SHH

Bird though she now is, still … she flees
the sight of men and light of day, and tries
to hide her shame in darkness, outcast
by all from the whole radiant sky.

Ovid, *Metamorphoses* II, 593–5

be still
you need stillness to know the night
which roosts treeless
above words or music
charm-proof

an owl
perched on Athena's left shoulder
swivels its head
and scans the goddess's
blind spot

its eyes
like two pilgrims renounce the near
sky's radiance
for focus on distant
objects

its ears
give up symmetry to funnel
soundwaves into
skullcaves from the lined-up
target

its wings
mastering slo-mo float along
velveted plumes
coasting down to make the
capture

Ovid
forefinger across lips mistook
its stealth for shame
and ignored the talons'
steel grip

adepts
of Athena's cousin Lakshmi
advised eating
owl eyes to navigate
the dark

Both west
and east were blind to mimicry
the mirroring
of snow by snowy owl
of tree

by wood-
owl the camouflage that reflects
our inner night
unmagicked and starless
the who

They fly from him ... poised on wings. One flies
    to the woods ...
their feathers are stained with blood.
                        Ovid, *Metamorphoses* VI, 667–70

Out of the throat of darkness
shadow-swaddled plumage
a streaked brown eminence
on streaked brown branch
audible light rises
fullness of iridescent sound
overspilling upwards

not Philomel because
not a cry of terror
pain grief or relief
at escape but song
fountaining from the calm
moon-brightened pool
between your folded wings

not Philomel because
welling up not after
but before wordful tongues
song needing no lyrics
instantly transposing
heart's joy in breathing
onto voice's pulse

the true metamorphosis
not a fledge of grounded
to winged but transformation
of your leaf-slight flesh
into forest-wide
song as high as trees'
night-steeped crowns

Nightingale because
you outface the chill
gales of night with a few
feathers and shivers of air

if we lose you we have
only the night
to face alone

ROUNDS

While the boy stretched out pleading hands ...
   and sought to
throw his arms around her neck, Procne smote him
   with a knife
between breast and side.

Ovid, *Metamorphoses* VI, 639–41

Not the straight thrust of Procne's knife
that one-way ticket for Itys
   nor the thrustings of Tereus
   freighted with terror and anguish
for helpless Philomela splayed
like a butcher's spatchcocked turkey

but circling marks the swallow's flights
from the long ellipsis over
   the Sahara and back each year
   to her thousand short return trips
when *la rondine* does the rounds
between riverbank and nest site

mouth filled with mud her beak will tamp
into place to form the smooth rim
   of a cup shape emerging from
   her mind's eye like the clutch of eggs
itself still no more than notion
opening from body-darkness

into light under the eave's wing
each dappled oval blossoming
    into a round mouth widening
    to plead for life the swallow's mouth
holds after harvesting the air
and offers as tender reply

while from the mayhem of sharp night-
mare where Procne hatched in our mind-
    darkness we look up towards rafters
    where the swallow has built a nest
in barn or shed or hip-roofed porch
and in the human spirit-house.

KINGFISHERS CATCH FIRE

*Still do they mate and rear their young; and for seven
peaceful days in the winter season Alcyone broods upon
her nest floating upon the surface of the waters. At such
a time the waves of the sea are still.*

Ovid, *Metamorphoses* XI, 744–7

Like parents who would keep their children
    free from the perishings of time
we dream heritage and habitat
    to lift you from a mortal world
tracing your shimmer to a far star
    your nest to unanchored floating

in stilled seas of myth while like us you
    hunger grow up give birth and die
no Alcyone but a common
    kingfisher yet we can't resist
draping your name in robes borrowed from
    our own throned blue-veined demigods

your blue a feathery scattering
    of light the iris of your eye
no rainbow but a brown hollow dark
    as the earthen riverbank nest
carved out with the same needle-nosed beak
    that will nourish hungry nestlings

whose bodies huddle together blind
    and featherless made of the same
earthen fabric as ours and whose eyes
    will open to air light water
the minds behind them knowing no myth
    aflame with being who they are

They hung in the air, magpies, the noisy scandal
of the woods ... in their feathered form their old-time gift
of speech remains, their hoarse garrulity,
their boundless passion for talk.

Ovid, *Metamorphoses* V, 676–8

Why do we hate them so when once
they were our dressed-for-dinner darlings
    shimmer of blue green purple bronze
dancing along black jacket feathers

    name a nicknamed diminutive
of Marguerite the tweeting sweeties
    pied like Dominican friars
their chatter deemed *jolly* by Chaucer

    cherished as neighbours by farmers
for strutting through barnyards to rid them
    of rodents and insects or pluck-
ing ticks from the backs of grazing sheep

    the noisy scandal of the woods
fits those who think it sport to kill "game"
    and would blame a magpie's hungry
ardour for depleting their larder

    e.g., Baron Winstanley who
addressing Parliament called magpies
    "thieving and murderous" vermin
and pushed for "capital punishment"

although their thievery is pure
mythology their nests humbly un-
     blinged built of twigs anchored in mud
and lined with grass not purloined coinage

     We hate them so because they do
what we do only better working
     in teams playing games even grieving
banding together to mob raptors

     bonding for life and on cold nights
bundled by hundreds in conifers
     to keep in body heat their broods
helpless and blind demanding receiving

     complete devotion from this pair
who are warbling softly now and who
     in their brief lives have earned the old-
time gift of speech and the gift of wings

AND A PARTRIDGE

Daedalus envied the lad and thrust him down headlong
*   from the sacred citadel ...*
But Pallas, who favours the quick of wit, caught him up
*   and made him a bird,*
and clothed him with feathers in mid-air. His old quick-
*   ness of wit passed*
into his wings and legs.

Ovid, Metamorphoses VIII, 250–5

Not fast enough dear partridge
to keep the egomaniac line
of Daedalus from pushing you
    off the edge of the world

Pallas outfitted you
with kit to thrive in wildest woods
suit of ground-hugging camouflage
    to baffle airborne foes

brave heart to run at earth-
bound claws and teeth and should that fail
the largest clutch of any bird
    to fly free when you're lunch

yet fewer raspy calls
ring through the undergrowth each year
the horseshoe marking on your chest
    target practice for fate

or curse of Daedalus
words hurled in envy of your wings
which did not melt unlike the ones
    he waxed for his doomed son

    his kind then mocked your flight
by naming you after your flat-
ulent (part-part-part) takeoff sound
    and rendering fatal

    the verb form of your name
to partridge meaning to hunt or shoot
your kind
           unless Pallas provide
    safe perch in a pear tree

He turned in flight, but was amazed to find
himself running
more swiftly than his wont, and saw wings sprout out upon
his body ... he pecked at the rough oak-trees with his
hard beak
and ... took the colour of his bright red mantle.

Ovid, *Metamorphoses* XIV, 388–93

In threads the bright red mantle of
    the morning sun passed through
    needle-eyes of the leaves
and cooling to green stitched itself

into the tree's living fabric
    stretching along branches
    or closeted among
roots in the subsoil to exchange

messages on a fungus web
    with siblings settling in
    for hundred-year-long naps
some never waking from heartwood

immured in darkness until tomb-
    looting beetles explored
    their cells and woodpecker's
keen ears picked up the theft and keen

beak battered light into the gloom
  transforming banked fire stored
  in the black beetle's core
quickened along a flickering tongue

and fanned by outsized ardent heart
  to plumed shafts fountaining
  from the bird's ridged brow to
the blazing sunrise of his crown

PEREGRINE

Now as a hawk, friendly to none,
he vents his cruel rage on all birds
and, suffering himself,
makes others suffer, too.

Ovid, *Metamorphoses* XI, 344–5

While you ply air's invisible
high seas we trawl for likenesses

your cupped wing a wind-filled sail
on cloud shoal swept by feathered keel

the shimmer of your muscled strokes
immersed fins navigating blue

or in your upsurge-arc-cascade
the liquid element itself

May flow and vector release you
from trammels of comparison

to be all peregrine falcon
emerged from tree-bark camouflage

not as falconer-unhooded
capturer to be recaptured

but fledged with wildness casting off
the oak branch perch like last year's moult

Dismantle in your swoop the mottled
secondaries we've pinned on you

from our wardrobe of cruelty
tricking out hunger pangs as hate

tagging as *hawk* those of our flock
who lust for blood of their own breed

while you with no more malice than
a raindrop plunge from heights of need

Indifferent to ownership
you're most content stretched out on shared

air among thinning sheets of cloud
your nest no custom-woven orb

of swatches flown in thread by thread
but a hollow scraped from loose grit

to hold the frail clutch of eggs
on a cliff's edge or high-rise ledge

You live most ardent in the deep
hearth of your telescopic eye

where clarities eight times as keen
as ours kindle and flare and give

rise to fresh bursts of earth or sea
which in their turn quench and recede

to the far corners of your globe
while you wing past their guttering wake

SONG AND DANCE

No feathered pinions uplift them, yet they sustain
themselves on transparent wings. They ... utter
only the tiniest sound. Houses,
not forests, are their favourite haunts.
                    Ovid, *Metamorphoses* IV, 410–14

At first they sought shelter there
millions of lifetimes before

human voices echoed through
caves later given back to

these winged refugees who'd fled
snapping jaws in the forest

The resonant limestone walls
became a recital hall

amplifying tiny sounds
from throats hanging upside down

piping their high-pitched greetings
these felt-covered sacks of song

Their voices became their eyes
navigating the darkness

more deftly than any bird
thin-boned wings sweeping upwards

the alert oversized ears
and panache of Fred Astaire

Light flashed behind them reveals
a Venice of red canals

flowing through wings more cape-like
than butter- or dragon-fly

a thousand beats per minute
no vampire's this dancing heart

HERALD

Worms that weave their white cocoons
on the leaves of trees (a fact
well known to country-folk) change
into funereal butterflies.

Ovid, *Metamorphoses* XV, 372–4

1

You might expect fanfare Ta Da
this herald parts the chrysalis
and four enameled wings emerge

but soft flutter is the waveband
on which a butterfly broadcasts
its tessellated messages

in keeping with the small spindly
body between spread coats of arms
that rolled-up-scroll holdover from

an earlier leaf-munching time
before the transformation to
this airborne sipper of nectar

2

Does its antennaed head still hold
a dream of undulating feet
or is this not makeover but

a birth announcement on a leaf
that death has wiped entirely clean
old body given up to air

new body breathing in the air
and circle on unfurling wing
no pretend-eye but the herald's

sign for our ring-shaped play where life
bows out sorrow-cloaked till sorrow's
tatters part for new life ta da

BESS BEETLE WOODNOTES

Old Cerambus ... by the aid of the nymphs borne up
into the air on wings ... when the heavy earth
had sunk beneath the overwhelming sea,
escaped Deucalion's flood undrowned.

Ovid, *Metamorphoses* VII, 353–6

They fly now on wings of less
vaulting mellifluousness
humbly reluctant to rise
Cerambus their ancestor
having been brought down to size
after thinking his singing
put him on par with the gods

Chastened lest fresh flood waters
drown larval sons and daughters
they live arked in fallen logs
their sharp-pointed mandibles
carving cursive passages
whose chiselled scraps they nibble
and feed offspring whose lives are

constant metamorphosis
like human children only
in colour-coded stages
from whitest innocent age
through emerging adult red
to fully grown ebony
with wings used less for flying

than for communicating
in plucked harplike rotation
a language of singing speech
whose notes wingless larvae reach
by letting leg glide on leg
in fiddle-like harmony
with their elders' melody

which rings through galleries drowned
in darkness a lifesaver
for beetle generations
called *bess* from *baiser* the sound
their music makes to our ears
as it turns their work to play
kiss-kissing the night away

Forthwith her hair, touched by the poison, fell off,
and with it both nose and ears ... the slender fingers
clung to her side as legs; the rest was belly.
Still from this she ever spins a thread.

Ovid, *Metamorphoses* VI, 140–5

1

Now she builds a world in the air living
   on what alights wrapping it
   in the same white silk she spins
to pave the lanes circling within her orb

She acts out the same play in which we're cast
   eating what earth offers us
   her spinnerets like our minds
drawing meaning from the meanest matter

Her large bellied body pregnant with silk
   reminds us gut reactions
   matter more than vague notions
spinning around inside a tiny head

2

Just as she won the wrath of Athena
   when she spun colourful tales
   of mortals seduced by gods
hiding inside skin or under feathers

So she one-ups her human rivals in
   the art of weaving drawing
   out a lighter stronger silk
than ever slender human finger spun

When she has opened her last woven map
   travels done eight legs draw in
   beneath silk's extinguished source
a darkened sun our bright world spins around

III

Earthbound Song

SIXTEEN HANDS

She clearly whinnied and her arms became legs
and moved along the ground ... Now was she changed
alike in voice and feature; and this new wonder
gave her a new name as well.

Ovid, *Metamorphoses* II, 668–75

Looking down from a maned head perched
like a flower on its thin-boned stem
the largest eye of any animal
that walks the earth cannot see back

to where her kind were weaponized
and ridden into rows of troops
or hauled a wooden-wheeled pumper
towards some inferno's white-hot eye

much less back to the first horse strapped
between ploughshafts or underneath
a saddle or to where clasped legs
of that barebacked rider we see

on the cave wall hugged her ribcage
but when she stands still and her eyes
close for the short naps horses take
she might dream herself back into

the fox-svelte form she took before
the outsized cultivar we bred
shook the ground and before we took
her measure counting human hands

and burned our brand into raw hide
that later shod our feet as we
the most ingenious predator
devoured the wild horse from within.

The father of the gods ... changed the men
  to ugly animals ...
that they might be unlike human shape and yet seem
  like them.
He shortened their limbs, blunted and turned back
their noses, and furrowed their faces with deep wrinkles.
                    Ovid, *Metamorphoses* XIV, 91–6

Would the mother of the gods have done that
or did it take paterfamilias
to make a monkey
                out of the monkey

as when he snatches one newborn nursing
from the warm breast and forces a tube down
its throat to pump drugs
                        into the young gut

or vaccinates the short-limbed body with
disease or drills its scalp and skull to screw
metal fetters into
                that furrowed brow

so it won't move during an induced stroke –
eyeball removed to block blood to the brain –
followed by fitness tasks
                    to gauge damage

while before mutilation the monkey's
eye watched its god and imitated its
body language as all
                    we primates do

mirror-neurons in monkey brains and ours
fostering mimicry so one might feel
as others feel
                    the pull of empathy

PIGGYBACKING

(I am ashamed to tell, yet will I tell)
I began to grow rough with bristles, and ... to bend
forward with face turned entirely to the earth.
I felt my mouth hardening into a long snout.
                    Ovid, *Metamorphoses* XIV, 279–83

Of all things to be ashamed of
Macareus you choose your change
from man to pig as if sacking
the Cicones' city and then
raping their women needed no
apology not to mention
the slaughterhouse you made of Troy

You're not alone making piggy
a scapegoat to be cast out to
the wilderness its porcine back
laden with the peccadilloes
of the neighbourhood and saddled
with the added charge of rolling
happily in its excrement

We exorcise our demons by
projecting human blemishes
onto the pink skins of fellow
creatures our messes morphing to
a pig's breakfast our gluttony
pigging out on potato chips
our nonsense a heap of *pigshit*

though we have learned that pigs are clean
animals with sensitive snouts
self-aware and moved by joyful
or depressing music and that
unlike people who piggyback
on them they fly on quickened wings
of empathy for other souls

The king himself ... gaining the silent fields,
howls aloud, attempting in vain to speak ...
His garments change to shaggy hair, his arms
to legs. He turns into a wolf.

Ovid, *Metamorphoses* I, 23–7

No fields are silent to those
who live in them as we do not ·
   A deer's ears twitch at the crunch
of footfall on leaf-fall too far
   for the net of human sense
to trap and an owl ear catches
   a mouse's tiny scurry

We lack the ultrasonic
range to tap the conversations
   crickets have beyond their chirp
or eavesdrop on a lone stonefly
   drumming on its abdomen
to awaken the attention
   of a potential partner

Yet our presumption over-
took our limits when we tried to
   take out the grey wolves and up-
set the balance of the forest's
   symphony their surplus prey
nibbling riverbanks to deserts
   leaving smaller mouths to starve

We misheard the wolfish howl
as deranged speech turning a deaf
    ear to its orchestration
of pitch and volume and a blind
    eye to subtle sign language
written in stiffened leg tensed lip
    and the long tail's semaphores

    and ignored resemblances
to our own kind their extended
    families the readiness
of pairs to adopt orphaned pups
    the agitation spreading
like a virus through the whole pack
    when one of its members dies

With our eyes swaddled in red
riding hoods and our ears unnerved
    by the cry of wolf how could
we know how large its soul without
    dissecting the beast never
letting ourselves get near enough
    to hear the great heart beating

48

UPON THY BELLY

He felt his skin hardening and scales growing on it,
while iridescent spots besprinkled his darkening body.
He fell prone upon his belly, and his legs
were gradually moulded together into one.

Ovid, *Metamorphoses* IV, 577–80

We fear them because they are close
to the earth and we like to think
of ourselves as above it all
spun from day-gleam and night-sparkle

abhorring their encounters with
humus that will claim our corpses
a threat they face veiled in thin scales
their only visors see-through lids

their bodies tapered frugally –
no paired appendages, one lung –
the lithe forked tongue no token of
duplicity but sensitive

tester of airborne trafficking
that escapes our bodies' radar
the sidewinding locomotion
no bellyflop but a headfirst

horizontal dive into streams
of ground-wind in the low countries
beneath feet which are too intent
on haste to swerve from lines we take

as we go upon our bellies
filling them with forests draining
lakes bulldozing mountains our jaws
opening far wider than theirs

what would we give to be able
to moult crawling out of our selves
the old skin breaking near the mouth
on something newer and brighter

THE EYES HAVE IT

It is their delight to live in water;
now to plunge their bodies quite beneath
the enveloping pool ... now to swim upon the surface ...
Now also their voices are hoarse, their inflated throats
  swell up.

Ovid, *Metamorphoses* VI, 370–7

You know them only skin-deep
slime-jacketed skin sticky
and repulsive to your eyes
as the bulbous throbbing throats'
husky ejaculations

to your ears. If you looked through
their eyes you would read *escape*
from capture on slippery skin
and listen to lullabies
rising clear from sweet-voiced throats.

See how their pond's blue planet
sports the same green cape as ours
and how a tadpole's journey
from guzzler to puffer maps
our old trail up from the sea.

Yet no metamorphosed prince
can draw breath under water
the way a frog's skin siphons
air from a muddy pond floor
and no human eye can see

three hundred sixty degrees.
Behind their clear shields these eyes
take in water land and sky
undistracted by story
totally focused on now.

LIONHEARTED

Oh, how often, when she could have passed him,
did she delay and after gazing long
upon his face reluctantly leave him behind!
                    Ovid, *Metamorphoses* X, 661–2

The female lion has the larger heart
(a quarter more by weight) and even did
before a spiteful goddess changed the girl's
fingers to claws arms to forelegs and fixed
growls where soft words had risen from her throat.

The female lion has the larger heart
and Atalanta showed the courage of
a lion when she (defying omens
that marriage would undo her) left the race
to catch love apples from Hippomenes.

The female lion has the larger heart
hunting with other females and sharing
catches with the entire pride unlike
nomadic males who roam to claim their own
territory and covet their own kills.

The female lion has the larger heart
which jealous Venus must have known and known
the male's phallus has backward-pointing spines
that rake the female's womb as he withdraws
triggering ovulation and yet still

the female lion with her larger heart
nurtures their blind and helpless cubs moving
the brood to new dens safe from predators
lifting them by the nape of the neck one
cub at a time whether male or female.

TO THE DOGS

She, with hoarse growls ... barked when she tried
*   to speak ...*
And ... long remembering her ancient ills,
still howled mournfully along the Sithonian plains.
                    Ovid, *Metamorphoses* XIII, 567–71

We have been going to you for
fifteen thousand years and you have
been coming to us both trotting
down the path of evolution
long-married couple like Priam
and Hecuba before Troy fell

we teaching you to keep your fangs
zipped in polite cave company
you teaching us to follow tracks
leading to food on our wood plates
each learning to read the shorthand
scribbled across the other's face

so when Hecuba was transformed
into a dog her new coat fit
better than an ape's shaggy cape
or an orangutan's red threads
despite the fact that both were her
long-lost cousins from savannah

and Ovid erred interpreting
her barks as warped speech rather than
parts of a vocabulary
whose words turn deft variations
on intonation pitch and speed
too subtle for mere human ears

to catch lacking canine sharpness
in that sense as in night vision
and as in the legendary
olfactory capacity
that allows you to distinguish
one twin's footprint from its brother's

and to detect the odour of
a fingerprint on a glass slide
making the real Hecuba wish
she'd been metamorphosed sooner
than that cataclysmic midnight
to sniff out Greeks crouched in their horse.

IV

Roots of Song

THE SACRED GROVE

Straightway he calls for all that sea and land
and air can furnish; with loaded tables before him
he complains still of hunger; in the midst
of feasts seeks other feasts ... The more he sends
down into his maw the more he wants.

Ovid, *Metamorphoses* VIII, 830–4

Time has metamorphosed Ovid's
villain Erysichthus into
us compounding his offenses.
He took an axe to Demeter's
sacred grove felling her great oak
and the wood nymph who lived within

while we bulldoze forests to stuff
our maw with everything from oil
and beef to aphrodisiacs
oblivious to woodland lives
(not mythical but real) of winged
and web-footed creatures or to

the self-taught aerodynamics
of the tree's growing limbs probing
the canopy for light each leaf
an astrolabe sensing the sun's
angled trajectory each root
navigating dark seas of earth.

Every grove is sacred holding
hushed conversations with the wind
that passes over clear-cut land
(as once over Erysichthus
whose fate was to devour himself)
and holds our metamorphosis.

OAKED

As a bird, when it has caught its foot in
the snare ... flaps and flutters, but draws its bonds
tighter by its struggling; so ... these women,
fixed firmly ... had stuck fast, with wild affright.
                    Ovid, *Metamorphoses* XI, 72–6

Ovid got it wrong transplanting
the Maenads' fear from earlier
in the story to the moment
Dionysus in his role as
Lyaeus the Deliverer
from Care anchored their frenzied feet
in earth and turned them all to oak.

They welcomed being *fixed firmly*
and now their fresh-sprung branches stretched
leaves flapping with grateful applause
for liberation from the wild
winged monster Orpheus released
from the barred hollows of his lyre.

Invisibly that creature stole
into their ears and perching in
the highest rafters of their brains
dispatched commands for vocal cords
to strum along with lyre strings
then ordered toes to tap in time
and legs to leap in hectic step.

Those Maenads hankering to be
deep-rooted got their wish though hints
of music trauma linger in
worried bark bulbous misaligned
limbs clinging to dead leaves and in
their veins' bitter tannic acid.

WHITE LIES

Bark closed over her latest words ...
Still their tears flow on, and these tears,
hardened into amber by the sun,
drop down from the new-made trees.

Ovid, Metamorphoses II, 363–5

We tell ourselves each blob of resin
oozing from the white poplar's cracked bark
is a teardrop and make up stories
about grieving sisters so deeply
rooted in lamentation their raised
arms turn branches and their fingers twigs.

We have all known families like that
the brother impulsive and hell-bent
on disaster the mother doting
the father sunny but credulous
the whole lot so close-knit the slightest
breeze convulses each singular soul

and just as Clymene reaches out
to tear off the bark from her daughters'
bodies so we reach out to this tree
to bring it into the human fold
perhaps because unlike godly oaks
poplars are fast-growing and short-lived.

Romans planted *populus* around
their public meeting places
Greeks made shields from the lightweight white wood
and Leonardo's *Mona Lisa*
is painted on poplar though we know
our tears will never turn to amber.

A LESSON FOR THE GODS

When the heavenly ones came to this humble home and,
    stooping,
entered in at the lowly door, the old man
set out a bench and bade them rest their limbs,
while over this bench busy Baucis threw a rough covering.
                    Ovid, *Metamorphoses* VIII, 637–40

Jupiter and Mercury
ushered to a wooden bench
as in a one-room schoolhouse
sit goggle-eyed and speechless
never having learned the math
of love where two equals one

while Baucis and Philemon
each working for the other
perform their joint *pas de seul*
one reaching to the rafters
for firewood while the other
arches to gather foodstuffs

both navigating a stream
of small talk to keep their guests
entertained who in grateful
astonishment grant the pair
a boon (call it tuition)
and after opting to be

one in death as in life (a
choice softened by the gods to
oneness as double-trunked trees)
Philemon and Baucis are
unchanged by having been changed
for – as gods can never learn –

every one that is mortal
is quickened by an other
and while linden's heart-shaped leaves
dance with oak's fingery leaves
their roots embrace each other
in an earthly underworld

NOT WEEPING BUT LOOKING

And now, as his life forces were exhausted
by endless weeping, his limbs began to change
to a green colour ... and he became a stiff tree
with slender top looking to the starry heavens.
                    Ovid, *Metamorphoses* X, 136–40

And talking with sisters and brothers
          rows of green candles standing
rooted in conversation deeper
          than chatter of leaf and branch

once a loner Cyparissus in
          his centuries as cypress
has grown to value these rap sessions
          among rhizomes and along

the landlines of hyphae linking them
          and to value keeping his
eyes open if he wants to keep them
          from overflowing with tears

he and his green kin being watchful
          for each other with every
cellulose molecule their vision
          not holed up in skull pockets

but shared out over their whole bodies
          fast-growing and long-lived sweet-
smelling with some of their wood destined
          to sing inside harpsichords

do they see we plant them where we plant
   our dead not to raise ever-
green spires of mourning but to sow hope's
   candles in a place of tears

NEVERLANDISH TREE

Over my white neck the soft bark comes creeping,
and I am buried in its overtopping folds.
                              Ovid, *Metamorphoses* IX, 388–91

No bark-clad lotus tree grows in Homer's
        Land of Lotus-Eaters merely
flowers and their intoxicating fruit
        so Ovid's Dryope becomes
a tree that never was and you can see
        the poet pulling trunk and barked
branches from what begins as a water
        lily as if he wanted to
wish a lotus tree into existence

others have shared his urge to raise Homer's
        lowly flower to a tall tree
Herodotus posits the Libyan
        date-plum Polybius a fruit
tree in Tunis other ancients touting
        the Indian loquat with its
mildly sedative pips or the elm-like
        Mediterranean nettle
that sports small purple soporific drupes

and who would not have wanted to drowse in
        that narcotic shade where Homer
nodded Herodotus stretching the truth
        to make a hammock far from front
lines Polybius trying to forget
        the sack of Carthage and Ovid
climbing some tree remote from his disgrace
        and banishment longing to perch
in high branches and never never land

FASTNESS

She ran, and a light air flung her locks streaming
    behind her ...
he pursued at utmost speed ... so ran the god and maid.
                    Ovid, *Metamorphoses* I, 529–39

Daphne had always loved *the deep*
fastnesses of the woods where time
lingered longer among ancient
moss-fringed pillars of oak and beech
than among freshets rushing through
her father the river god's house.

She loved the leaves' slow unfurling
the way they evaded her eye's
reach by appearing not to move
as if those tongues had never learned
a language of minutes or hours
and only spoke in weeks and months.

She also loved the crowns' complete
indifference to the wind's urgings
how they just seemed to nod assent
to restless to-ing and fro-ing
but kept a steady course and steered
for the forest's sunlit harbours.

So she would not love Apollo's
love of speed his predilection
for the come-and-go of music
over the still designs of stone
or his thoughts' willing surrender
to an arrow flight of action.

Realizing she could not out-
run him she determined to out-
slow him pulse tide at low ebb breath
taken in and held in lungs that
kept it fingers stiff as waxwork
wooden toes anchored in the loam.

The laurel tree is slow-growing
its grain is fine its green ever
its picked leaves do not develop
full flavour until weeks later
for decades after laurel wood
is cut it will remain fragrant

GREEN MAGIC

Romulus … saw his spear-shaft …
suddenly putting forth leaves
and standing … with new-grown roots.
Ovid, Metamorphoses XV, 560–3

Garrick Ollivander will tell you
each wand has a personality

this wrinkled willow wand a mentor
and poet well versed in water lore

from living its fluent metaphors
bark picking up ripples from the stream

stream catching leaf-rustle cadences
spell of each each
                    transformed to other

Mentor because more than the stream that's
here today there tomorrow the tree

puts down its foot to hold headlong soil
back from the brink and teaches it to

stay and nurture willowy offspring
not plummet like a sorcerer's stone

magicked by Hollywood and sinking
beneath the waves
                              in a slow dissolve

Like Romulus filmed in slow motion
you can watch the brown skeleton of

a willow stick thrust into the ground
transform to a sapling within months

the stick its own water diviner
the sapling a cascade of green leaves

watch this magic and wonder whether
you can match your
                              mentor's thirst for life

UNDERGROWTH OVERACHIEVER

Or was it once allowed
to thee, Persephone,
to change a maiden's form
to fragrant mint?

Ovid, *Metamorphoses* X, 728–30

In her guise as the naiad Menthe
bent on honeying the sourest depths
mint staked a claim issuing fragrant

come-hithers like those invitations
we meet in our garden mint's wanton
runners tender underaged offshoots

mint's teen children childbirthing further
mint indiscriminately in sun
or shade mint even in the deepest

darkness of the underworld beside
the inky current of Cocytus
mint resolved to offset death's fetid

odours with the babyfresh scent of
mint and carry her campaign right to
the bed of Hades himself but not

reckoning on Persephone's wrath
the queen of the underlands fearful
of being usurped while away from

her mate on a summer holiday
banished mint to upperworld verges
where Hades' chariot never wheeled

but she could not stop mint from minting
quadruplets those fourfold pimpled leaves
sweetening forest understories.

Pan, when now he thought he had caught Syrinx,
instead of her held naught but marsh reeds ...
and while he sighed in disappointment, the soft
air stirring in the reeds gave forth ... sweet tones.
Ovid, *Metamorphoses* I, 705–9

She paused in the instant
of her transformation
to catch her breath catching
the wind's breath raising it
from fretful hum to song

in the swaying chamber
of a newly greened mouth
as her fluttering tongue
shaped harmonies from sound's
waves cresting the reed beds.

The metamorphosis
that followed hers took shape
when a mute bird's desire
for song wished the reed swept
by sound into his throat

where a reborn syrinx
plays on the set of pipes
arising from within
the feathered breast catching
a contented heart's beat.

BRIDGE

The bare-trunked pine with broad, leafy top,
pleasing to the mother of the gods,
since Attis, dear to Cybele, exchanged
for this his human form and stiffened in its trunk.

Ovid, *Metamorphoses* X, 103–5

Masts for tall sailing ships pit-props
for mine-shafts rafters telegraph
poles fence posts sleepers for railroads
dressers caskets baskets all these
human uses for you when you're
dead pine but what of living pine
pleased your earth mother Cybele

was the bridge you made of yourself
spanning many gaps and taking
many shapes the green-crowned pillar
an aqueduct drawing water
from lightless channels under rock
to sunswept canopy the ringed
calendar at your core linking

logged seasons past to ridged present
the upswept needles buttressing
each other against tides of wind
the way your mother's crown imaged
both the inchoate stone of black
meteoric iron at one
end of the line from wilderness

to settlement and the bronze walls
ringing the other end's harvest
or the way the hard residue
left when your resin is distilled
can when rubbed on a violin's
bow send music floating over
body neck fingerboard and bridge

V

Breath Marks

His skin is stripped off the surface ... blood flows down ...
all wept for him ... the fruitful earth ... caught those tears
and drank them deep into her veins. Changing these
   then to ...
Marsyas, the clearest river in all Phrygia.
                              Ovid, *Metamorphoses* VI, 387–400

of blood: disgusts Apollo still
            more than the spittle-dappled breath
            spewing from pan-pipes the creature
            musicks goading the god whose veins
            run with ichor's mirror-clearness
            whose lungs spurn the air Marsyas
            shares with mortal kind furred and fanged
                so accomplished strumming fingers
                pluck the skin from throbbing sinews

                     –   –   –

of tears: bears witness to the god's
            apartness as all those breathers
            mourn Marsyas fauns and satyrs
            nymphs and shepherds their tears hosting
            the same salt that swims through their blood
            legacy from the sea-source of
            life's mortal tree but not of the
                undying rootless Apollo
                hanging in air unsupported

                     –   –   –

of rain: washes tears into earth
            which ushers them through crevices

into underground horizons
brown sphere setting to sub-soil sub-
soil slipping into bedrock where
the slow embrace of gravity
filters fresh water drop by drop
    collecting into veins that feed
    the brown trunk's ramifying green

      –   –   –

of rivers: is all overflow
breaking from underground sources
to muscle its way over all
the mortal building-blocks limestone
of bones iron of blood salt of
tears in a throbbing cataract
calling with pan-pipes that outlast
    gods who are mere air breath condensed
    on the surface of some old hymn

Men saw thee as a youth, now as a lion ...
now a serpent whom men would fear to touch ...
often thou couldst appear as a stone ...
sometimes assuming the form of flowing water.
                    Ovid, *Metamorphoses* VIII, 732–6

As a teenager he stood in front
of his mirror and practised roaring
to scare off the locker-room vultures
the next time they picked up his gym bag
and alley-ooped it into the pool.

Grown he camouflaged his lisp into
a hiss his thin skin into sharp scales
his shyness borrowed a stealthy gait
from serpent-slither and an icy
handshake fronted a cold-blooded stare.

He confronted loss by studying
the impassive demeanor of stones
but none of them not igneous's
overcome meltdowns nor the oneness
he felt with the skeletal remains

of sedimentary nor stoic
metamorphic's pressure-resistance
worked and his composure decomposed
salt water wetting his once leonine now
grey mane as he aped the pose of sleep.

SO LET US MELT

Cyane ... nursed an incurable wound in her silent heart,
and dissolved all away in tears ... You might see her
   limbs softening ...
back and sides and breasts vanish into thin
watery streams ... and nothing is left that you can touch.
                              Ovid, *Metamorphoses* V, 425–37

And make no noise as we follow
   Cyane whose heart softens
at the rape of Persephone
   and reflects that sister's pain
so fully Cyane becomes
   mirroring water the blue
stream of self dissolved in other

as a mirroring other once
   gave shape to our infant self
since only from the gentle gaze
   of eyes that can melt in tears
do we receive the gift of love
   that opens our senses to
the feeling of being ourselves

that country whose underground streams
   we explore on rafts fashioned
of fellow beings like the hugged
   soft-furred bear guarding our crib
or the real cat whose pleased murmurs
   our voicebox appropriates
to breathe out wordless contentment

for everything alive is borne
   on a river of matter
changing from one identity
   to another Cyane
then water then Persephone
   who melts in turn
and in deep time resurfaces

and what connects us along with
   the very act of changing
is the riptide of empathy
   which murmuring a oneness
at the heart of all our changes
   runs counter to the current
and is nothing that you can touch

FRANKINCENSE

Straightway the body, soaked with the celestial nectar,
melted away and filled the earth around
with its sweet fragrance. Then did a shrub of frankincense
with deep-driven roots, rise slowly through the soil.
Ovid, Metamorphoses IV, 252–5

Wishful thinking Ovid not even
Phoebus could bring Leucothoë back
straightway to fragrance if not to life
under the earth her outraged father
covered her with on discovering
that she was sleeping with the sun god.

We all sleep and wake up with Phoebus
following in his chariot tracks
day by day but in a deeper time
marked by the lifting and levelling
of seas and mountains he orchestrates
a dance of carbon and oxygen

air to breath back to air do-si-do
rock to eggshell to birdwing to bone
to rock once more and skip to my lou
nothing *straightway* a slow circle-dance
life passed on from dancer to dancer
each bowing out as they pass it on.

Ovid called it metamorphosis
and must have surmised that frankincense
grew in harsh regions beset by strife
and poverty driving roots into
solid rock its lemony fragrance
sweetening the bitterness of loss.

TRANSPOSED

A chill stole through her fingers and toes, and her flesh
was pale and bloodless ... so did a deadly chill
little by little creep to her breast, stopping
all vital functions and choking off her breath ...
Her neck was changed to stone, her features had hardened.
                    Ovid, *Metamorphoses* II, 823–31

In earlier days she would melt
with pity at another's pain
some legends avowing she threw
herself on the sacrificial
pyre of her sister Chthonia
the same legends that give her name
as Agraulos ("countryside flute").

"Aglauros" in most accounts met
a cooler end after envy
of her sister Herse's romance
with Mercury made her blockade
the threshold to Herse's chamber
arousing the wrath of the god
whose wand turned Aglauros to stone.

Chilled by her sister's happiness
and deaf to Mercury's love songs
her heart was stone even before
her flesh thickened as stiff as bone
and blood froze into porphyry
transposing the countryside flute's
arpeggios to a lower key

where it awaits an arrangement
in the deep time of the future
when stone will pulse with life again
as mountain ranges ebb and flow
and the countryside flute so long
confined and set to hard labour
will play its melting harmonies.

STONES AND BONES

And the stones – who would believe it unless
ancient tradition vouched for it? – began …
to grow soft slowly, and softened to take on form.
                    Ovid, *Metamorphoses* I, 400–2

Very slowly but since Pyrrha
and Deucalion are figures
of myth they can walk at the same
pace glaciers or tectonic plates
shift slow as a billion migrant
songbird journeys stacked end to end

and the stones they throw behind them
can roll in mountain streams and break
down into earth-crumbs that eons
of sun quicken the dry ones bones
the moist ones flesh veins in the rock
becoming arteries' red flow.

Not only "ancient tradition"
but the air vouches for it too
after shuffling around as wind
chanting random notes finally
finding a rhythm in the ins
and outs of counterpointed breath

and singing mouths can vouch for it
as tongues roam the craggy mountain
range of our teeth beneath the stone
roof of a labyrinthine cave
housing among winding branches
the nest where the music echoes

VI

Love Songs

SONG ON PAPER

I seem to see you already swimming near
and now to feel your wet arms about my neck,
and now to throw about your dripping limbs
the accustomed coverings, and now to warm
your bosom clasped to mine.
            Ovid, *Heroides* XIX ("Hero to Leander"), 59–62

    The nib leaves its wake of ink
on the white sea beneath the star
    of her flickering candle.

    Hero will guide it the way
Leander's strokes inscribe the waves
    from his sandy shore to hers.

    More windswept than any flag
ruffling on the pen's little mast
    her thoughts break from the parchment

    and like Orpheus follow
a thin black trail aglow with flame
    as it spills out its letters

    each tilted spar or oval
beckoning to her eyes hands heart
    to make the absent present

    make currents of silent song
strong enough to bring Leander
    striding breathless up the beach

make *here* dissolve in a sea of
there where she would find him after
the ink's mirrored starlight dries.

When in truth I can be seen
as well as see, by your glance
you … give me heart, and make me strong.
                   Ovid, *Heroides* XVI ("Leander to Hero"), 93–4

As landing lights can mean both one
   on a runway and one attached
to an aircraft so the eyes that
   guide Leander shorewards are his
own and Hero's his taking in
   the light hers radiate when hers
      harbour visions of his approach.

At closer range he hopes to find
   himself in Hero's eyes and she
herself in his where otherwise
   each lacks a mirror to surround
the flesh tones of each wide-eyed face
   and set within a rainbow frame
      a blackness deeper than the night.

Yet dual portraits falsify
   a oneness deeper than the reach
of gloss or flesh Leander's ink
   affirming he and Hero share
a single heart she gives to him
   to fire his way across cold waves
      that keep two bodies separate.

Leander the lone swimmer's love
    for Hero powers every stroke
Hero the beacon that casts rays
    of love over a distant beach
love in their eyes will be enough
    to land them in each other's arms
    or so he writes at letter's end.

TOUCH

I will come to be thy comrade whithersoever
thou dost call, whether that which, alas, I fear,
shall come to pass or whether thou shalt still survive.
   Ovid, *Heroides* XIII ("Laodamia to Protesilaus"), 163–4

   Her tongue trips over
    the words the whithers whethers
and whiches unable to find

   the path between teeth
    and lips as remote from his
touch as the pen that hesitates

   and blurs the *l*'s of
    will into meaningless *d*'s
because the fingers holding it

   would rather be held
    by his hand out of reach now
across Aegean seas she tried

   to bridge by dipping
    toes into waves knowing
his foot would be wading ashore

   at the other end
    but the water's touch chilled her
as never his so she ran back

to the house and sank
her face into his tunic
yet its weave fresh-washed no longer

let her breathe him in
now she writes and tells herself
his hand will caress the parchment

hers now holds his eyes
embrace the strokes of her pen
but then is a sea's breadth from now

and when she closes
her own eyes they wake in the
grip of a night untouched by sleep.

SONG ON PAPER II

I can write to you and your dear eyes
roam over my words, your dear eyes.
                    Freya to Helmuth James, 26 October 1944

Peregrine-keen eyes glide over landscapes
            of each other's letters
her script a freshly planted field with ink-
            shoots barely surfacing

from tiny even rows – his looking sown
            earlier fuller-leaved
casting thicker shadows on ridged rows that
            crest like waves of hillside

each pair of eyes sharpened from years of reading
            the other's acres
whether on paper or in an exchange of
            glances from *dear eyes*

where viewer becomes view and lush valleys
            of I-love-you open
beneath a fringed lid and behind the dark
            centre of a rainbow

and whether shaped by hand or lips words swooped-on
            and devoured become
part of each watcher deeper than lustre on
            plumage or pupil

a thinning down of boundaries until one
        impulse moves freely
between two bodies each reaching a space
        beyond the body's reach

as when two separate tree perches are inter-
        twined under the earth
or when with eyes hooded in sleep dreams dissolve
        earthworks to canals.

AIRBORNE

Since you're also at this place, I thought
maybe we could keep reading together.
                    Helmuth James to Freya, 28 November 1944

The guards would have been mystified if they had read
            this letter which
Helmuth's friend the prison chaplain smuggles out past
            bars and censors

this place in their eyes Helmuth's cell too small for an
            also where he
perches blanket-draped atop his desk above the
            stone floor's damp cold

they can hear his whistling but fail to see he's flown
            beyond the nest
one of those birds like dove or lark that trill and quaver
            on the wing

his flight assisted by splayed rows of buoyant black
            on a white page
which lift him past bomb-raked Berlin this morning to
            Jerusalem

where Christ is schooling Pharisees in loving neighbours
            as themselves
which Matthew wrote down at *this place* where Helmuth
    plans
            to meet Freya

but now a thought-vortex propels his mind to a
                    recalled report
of two hundred Greek "neighbours" killed in reprisal
                    for one German

and helpless now to give the help he tried to he
                    more urgently
changes the place where eyes must light
                    to First Corinthians thirteen

Helmuth no mountain-bred eagle or peregrine
                    nothing unless
he whistles the ground-nesting mourning dove's love song
                    of charity.

KEEPERS

I covered up the bees and hid
the letters in the hives.
Freya to Helmuth James, 24–6 October 1944

Think of it as an act
of resistance after spiders
    inject the German flag
with venom Freya keeps sweetness
    alive setting out fresh
frames for bees to fill with honey.

The bees' song-and-dance act
captivates them both the solo
    performance that inspires
a chorusing swarm to follow
    to blossom-fields of vetch
or trefoil and later the soft

hum of contentment as
a benign metamorphosis
    converts the flowers' dust
into growing bodies of bees
    who know sweetness and would
die were they to wield their venom

but when spider venom
seeps into Gestapo eyes she
    hives away filled frames of
his letters heavy with traces
    of flower species saved
from the mowing machine's toothed blade.

    After the blade finds him
Helmuth's letters absorb so much
    sweetness from their refuge
the honey can sustain Freya
    who keeps them at bedside
through sixty-five more years of life.

IN AND OUT OF TIME

Nine months of my imprisonment ... you will have carried
your worries and fear for me as long as you carried
your little sons. If I must die, then I hope that
through these nine months I'll be reborn to you.
          Helmuth James to Freya, 17 October 1944

In prison and running out of time he still
measures time less by the clock than by nature's cycles
birth of children blossom of lilac and magnolia

    senses Freya's monthly onset
      sees that like the August scent
  of lindens he will not outlast winter

and knows that seeing death in the farthest distance
is a gift denied lilacs or lions and balanced
by the sister gift of seeing beyond the bounds

    of time sharp sightings taken through
    the lens of the heart as when
  walking in thought he feels her hand in his

and the same eyes that lift him into her world
remake the round world's zoned times into one sea
the same water lapping Shanghai Sydney and Table
  Mountain

    the water babies cresting hand
      in hand with one another
  born and reborn from an endless mothering sea

Desperate at the thought that your old train set
might be nothing but a wreck ... we set it up ...
it turned out that it is wonderful ...
the locomotive manages to go backward.
                    Freya to Helmuth James, 24–5 December 1944

Fifty years after that Christmas
    (Helmuth's last) Freya's eyes will
follow the tracks laid by her pen
    (the black ink browned now) going

backwards to earlier stations
    along the line once more where
rumble of toy locomotive
    subsides into song of hives

Helmuth asking if they should move
    finished comb from twenty-nine
to famished eighteen or just look
    after the best and strongest

traditional practice with bees
    only now applied he adds
to humans his thoughts haunted by
    frail flesh hived in cattle cars

farther back brings happier scenes
    air over the tracks scented
with freshly ploughed fields and lily
    of the valley in the woods

her nose twitches as she follows
    the line but it is her hand
that derails her reaching out for
    his as they walked side by side

her happiest destination
    Stockholm never visited
except through his letters pure him
    with her looking through his eyes

at this city set on trackless
    water where the tide like a
sower transformed into water
    spreads fresh future every day

Isaiah ... is too elevated above human woes ...
I greatly prefer Daniel and Solomon and the Psalms ...
because I'm simply a little blade of grass
eagerly seeking and obtaining solace and help.
                    Helmuth James to Freya, 31 December 1944

On grey days with less
  than a month to live he hears
St Paul whisper through his own voice
  that the treasure's name is Light

  which cannot reach him
  an earthen vessel of flesh
living with his dark thoughts confined
  in a vessel barred and locked

  and yet not alone
  his thoughts so married to hers
they wear the same outfits of words
  it is Freya who lifts him

  from the *miry clay*
  of Psalm 40 a *new song*
in his mouth Freya who lives in
  his heart Love another name

  for Light that will play
  unconfined by the earthen
vessel's walls over the Berlin
  sewage fields to which Himmler

consigns cremated
bodies of the convicted
and offer help and solace to
a little blade of grass mid-

way on its journey
from earth to sky bright as a
musical sawblade vivid in
sunshine singing with the wind

VII

The Chorus

VII

The Chorus

AN OH

Under the hide of me
there's an oh, such a hungry
yearning burning inside of me.
                        Cole Porter, "Night and Day"

Song gives him what life withholds an Oh
that interrupts his musical line
rounded lips breathing out the *hungry*
yearning never to be spoken of
the *burning* under his ash grey suit

kindled by an instinct that he sees
circus animals in his home town
free to unleash the chimps the trained fleas
all doing it the only act left
for him the shuffle of a sad clown

stumbling from the ring's deserted O
after another vain performance
another dreamt forever finding
its rhyming end with never under
the lost O of a withering moon

song transforming the shiver of pain
into a rhythm the rise and fall
of hope traced in a sequence of notes
poured out through a round of brass whose lip
draws from our lips an ecstatic Oh

Who could ask for anything more?
                    Ira Gershwin, "I Got Rhythm"

Ira could after George's death
left him brotherless and untuned
the duets hushed between keyboard
and the desk drawn up beside it
the rhythm of decades broken

George's body having carried
out of this world a dance of hands
over white and black tiles a swoop
and sway of shoulder and torso
and their transformation into

the floating butterfly of song
Ira inheriting only
crows sitting on telephone wires
an unfinished page of black dots
abandoned on the music stand.

Longing to show undying love
knowing only a dance of words
that die though bodiless Ira
circles his love with rings of rhyme
the ancient spell to ward off time

but *stay* gives way to *day* and death
will not be checked by echoed breath
in a world where mountains crumble
rocky outcrops come tumbling down
and we like them are made of clay.

As George heard music in the heart
of noise Ira's lyrics let in
his age's migratory birds
the radio the telephone
their flights of song not here to stay
but here going a long long way.

is no mortal morphing into
torso-trunk arm-branch finger-leaf
    no body caught in mid-career
    although flight and transformation
seeded its twin identity
both living Newfoundland stage prop
    and ghostly I-beam rooted in
    the rubble of nine-eleven

these twins conjoin more closely in
audience minds than forest trees
    whose branches intertwine above
    and rootlets bind below the earth
or beams fused by flaming rivets
into a tower's square ribcage
    the tree branchless as a steel beam
    the beam sprouting a fresh green leaf

this *tree* was not the number *three*
in pilot language when the air
    traffic control tower's squawk code
    gave clearance seven-two-*tree*-five
for flight five-*tree*-niner to land
as Gander's airwaves filled with *trees*
    while New York City's air was filled
    with smoke from the burning towers

then the come-from-aways traded
cloud-turbulence for gentle waves
    of local dialect where *fear*
    lightens and falls from lips as *fair*
and your home is *where you longs to*
language that sings of open arms
    and prefigures an unfolding
    green from the once-felled spotlit trunk

CONNECTED

To be alive is to reach out
to an other as trees do through
their roots speeding electrical
and chemical message-bearers
from station to station along
an underground fungal network

or as honeybees do turning
the patterns of their dance into
words in a vocabulary
or reef squid shaping sentences
by flexing muscles that control
the colour patterns of their skin

in semaphores our eyes can trace
although our ears can never catch
high frequencies of moth-to-moth
or grasshopper-to-grasshopper
conversations or the low range
of the elephants' colloquies

so it is understandable
that the come-from-aways tied up
the internet and all land-line
connections round the clock like bats
singing to each other by name
to keep in touch in the darkness.

GIFTS FROM THE SWIFT

They must remind her of herself
if she looks down on them from cloud-
height those thirty-eight grounded planes
that owe their ancestry to her
    along with the cloud-cleaving scythes
    splayed behind their snub-nosed cockpits.

Would we have ever dreamt of flight
unless her edged cry raised our eyes
to the swoop and soar of those blades
as they shear the evening's blue silk
    yet leave its darkening waters
    seamless as when a magician's

assistant after being sawn
in two emerges one again
from the curtained box the swift still
more deft than we at living with
    conjuring her muscles making
    minute and impromptu tweakings

to stay abreast of waves on air's
unseen seas where our wings founder
without the cockpit instruments
that translate magic into math
    and where winged dreams when weaponized
    leave two tall boxes smoke-curtained.

Her own dream was her second gift
to us not magic but a glimpse
through clouds where swifts drift half asleep
of how we might move *weep weep weep*
  from downcast eye to lifted throat
  and turn it like hers into song.

TRANSFORMERS

We all are whether gills draw breath
from water lungs from air or both

like tadpole slipped into frogsuit
shucking the outgrown self from tooth

to tail during an afternoon
or caterpillars in cocoons

taking months to trade stubby limbs
for wardrobes from the cherubim.

The child turning an autobot
from car to humanoid is not

less metamorphic than the toy
and inside a changing body

as freshwater sees the yellow
eel take on its silvery glow

the soul to whom group games brought hurt
can bloom into an extrovert

A change of jacket in the play
makes Kevin the "come-from-away"

over into Garth the Gander
bus driver and when he hands a

fishing hat to his neighbour it
transforms Nick from a quiet Brit

to Doug the mouthy vet who when
hatless becomes Nick once again.

Like the actors breath by breath we
surrender selves we used to be

and take on fresh changes of *me*
like grasshoppers who wriggle free

from exoskeletal debris
time after time till rainbowy

wings flag the new identity
of one who's yet the same old *me*

but for the sense of empathy
that grows from knowing an other

inside one's own shell. So children
in their everyday play practice

the humanity that offered
kind community to Gander's

stranded refugees taking on
costume changes singing new songs.

CHALK

is an ambassador from deep
time whose sweep hand is the movement
of mountains drift of tectonic
plates epoch drip of stalactites

and deep time one of those cultures
where white is the garb of mourning
since chalk consists of the bodies
of countless single-celled creatures

who gave up their backbones and shells
to the seabeds from whose waters
they'd extracted the white calcite
to fabricate spines and houses

such as those on the Dover Fault
where two lovers think they have come
for *hold it* moments in the view
but what they see lies back beyond

all human love and frightens them
with the unfeeling face of stone
the mouth a trackless cave where no
echo has ever held a song

but this moment's consolation
is the gift chalked on a blackboard
at the school that housed these lovers
and their fellow come-from-aways

this sketch of a gander in flight
every feather detailed in chalk
which will soon be erased and dust
linger in the air like the songs
we sing to make our moment last

NEW SONGS

My mind is bent to tell of bodies
changed into new forms ...
from the world's very beginning even
unto the present time.

Ovid, *Metamorphoses* I, 1–4

Mote by mote the universe
recycles itself celestial
and earthly bodies the dust
that dazzled space millennia
ago as sun or star now
seeing rather than sending light
freshly reconfigured as
cowled eye of a great grey owl whose

orbed earways take in the swish
of a mouse's tail whose atoms
once stood tall in a cornfield
where ears you picked became part of
your own eye which now houses
like all the cells in your body
a little gallery of
symbiont bacteria in

transit between guest houses
all with doors open to the world's
      travellers each following
a different timetable from the
      marine microbe's ten-minute
lifespan to the bristlecone pine's
      five thousand years and counting
         as cells release piece after piece

of themselves surrendering
their bodies in fragments to be
      changed into new songs new worlds
of stars and pines and owls open
      the doors of your lungs breathe in
to make these yours and breathing out
      give your song in return to
         a world beyond the present time

"Minstrels": After being raped by Jupiter and changed into a heifer to avoid detection by Juno, Io was finally changed back into human form and was later worshipped as a goddess.

"Shh": Daughter of the King of Lesbos, Nyctimene unknowingly slept with her father and then fled to the forest, where she was changed into an owl by Minerva.

"Not Philomel," "Rounds": Philomel was raped by her brother-in-law Tereus, who then cut out her tongue. Communicating her story in a weaving, Philomel joined her sister Procne, who took revenge on Tereus by killing their son Itys and feeding his remains to Tereus. Fleeing his wrath, Philomel was changed to a nightingale and Procne to a swallow.

"Kingfishers Catch Fire": The gods rewarded the fidelity of Alcyone and Ceyx, who escaped death through a transformation into kingfishers. "Halcyon days" take their name from Alcyone, each year granted calm waters on which to build her nest.

"Black and White": The nine daughters of Pierus mocked and challenged the Muses to a song contest and were defeated and changed into magpies.

"And a Partridge": Jealous of the precocity of his nephew Perdix, Daedalus threw him from the sacred hill of Athena, who rescued the boy and changed him into a partridge.

"How Woodpecker Rekindled the Sun": The fidelity of Picus to Canens outraged jealous Circe, who transformed him into a woodpecker.

"Peregrine": Fierce Daedalion, maddened by Diana's murder of his daughter, threw himself from a cliff but was changed into a hawk by Apollo.

"Song and Dance": The three daughters of Minyas were changed into bats for being homebodies and ignoring the festival of Bacchus.

"Herald": *Funereal* because departed souls were sometimes imaged on tombstones as butterflies.

"Bess Beetle Woodnotes": Cerambus, the greatest singer-songwriter of his (mythical) age, was rescued from Deucalion's flood by the nymphs, but his vanity and scorn drove them to shrink him into a beetle.

"Silk Roads": Angered by Arachne's weavings, which depicted the scandalous behaviour of the gods, Athena turned her into a spider.

"Sixteen Hands": As punishment for dabbling in prophecy, Ocyrhoë was transformed into a heifer.

"Monkey See": Annoyed with the treacheries of the Cercopians, Jupiter turned them into monkeys.

"Piggybacking": A companion of Ulysses, Macareus had been turned into a pig by Circe until he was rescued.

"Wolfsbane": For his savage behaviour, King Lycaon was transformed by Jupiter into a wolf.

"Upon Thy Belly": As punishment for killing a serpent sacred to Mars, Cadmus was himself changed into a serpent.

"The Eyes Have It": For preventing the parched goddess Latona from drinking at their pool, a group of Lycian peasants was transformed into frogs.

"Lionhearted": The newlyweds Atalanta and Hippomenes, carried away by desire, made love inside a temple and were punished by being changed into growling lions.

"Oaked": My version of the story has the Maenads driven mad by the music of Orpheus and grateful to be transformed into oak trees, rather than being punished for contemptuously killing him.

"White Lies": Sisters of the perished Phaeton, the Heliades' ceaseless lamentation for him turned them into white poplars shedding tears of amber.

"Not Weeping but Looking": Cyparissus unwittingly killed a beloved stag. Begging that he might mourn forever, he was transformed into a cypress tree.

"Neverlandish Tree": Dryope plucked some blossoms of water-lotus to amuse her infant son and was punished by being changed into a lotus tree.

"The Wind Among the Reeds": "Syrinx" connotes both the reeds that form pan-pipes and a bird's organ of voice.

"Bridge": The earth mother Cybele was associated with both the unshaped black rock of a primitive landscape and the bronze walls of a settled town.

"The Flow": Marsyas lost a musical contest to Apollo, who unfairly proclaimed his lyre superior to the shepherd's pan-pipes and then punished Marsyas by flaying him alive and turning the carcass into a lyre or wind-harp.

"Stages of His Age": Proteus was able to metamorphose into many shapes.

"Frankincense": Orchamus buried his daughter Leucothoë alive for having slept with Apollo who, unable to revive her, transformed her into a shrub of frankincense.

"Song on Paper," "Landing Lights," "Touch": Hero and Leander, and Laodamia and Protesilaus, are four of Ovid's doomed epistolary lovers. Hero committed suicide after Leander drowned trying to swim to her across the Hellespont, and Laodamia killed herself on learning that Protesilaus was the first Greek to die in the Trojan War.

"Song on Paper II" through "Treasure in Earthen Vessels": These poems are based on letters written to each other by Freya and Helmuth James von Moltke during the year he spent in prison awaiting execution by the Nazis for high treason. Scion of a great Prussian military family, Helmuth James and his wife actively engaged in resistance against the Third Reich, helping Jews and dissidents to flee from Germany and implicated in the failed assassination attempt on Hitler in July 1944. Helmuth James was executed on 23 January 1945. See Freya and Helmuth

von Moltke, *Last Letters: The Prison Correspondence,
1944–45*, New York: New York Review Books, 2019.

"Airborne": Matthew 22:39: "Thou shalt love thy
neighbour as thyself." First Corinthians 13:2: "Though I
have the gift of prophecy, and understand all mysteries, and
all knowledge; and though I have all faith, so that I could
remove mountains, and have not charity, I am nothing."
Twelve days before his execution, Helmuth James wrote
to Freya that "You are my 13th chapter of 1 Corinthians.
Without this chapter, no human being is human."

"Treasure in Earthen Vessels": Corinthians 2:6–7: "For
God, who commanded the light to shine out of darkness,
hath shined in our hearts, to give the light of the knowledge
of the glory of God in the face of Jesus Christ. But we have
this treasure in earthen vessels, that the excellency of the
power may be of God, and not of us." Psalm 40:1–2: "He
brought me up also out of an horrible pit, out of the miry
clay, and set my feet upon a rock, and established my
goings. And he hath put a new song in my mouth."

"An Oh": The social mores of his time and place forced
Cole Porter to keep secret his identity as a gay man. Porter's
"Let's Do It" observes that "even educated fleas do it."

"Our Love Is Here": Ira Gershwin wrote the lyrics to
"Love is Here To Stay" – the last music George Gershwin
completed before his death – as a tribute to his brother:
"Together we're going a long, long way / In time the
Rockies may crumble / Gibraltar may tumble / They're
only made of clay / But our love is here to stay."

"This Tree" through "Chalk" allude to various elements of the Canadian musical *Come From Away*, by Irene Sankoff and David Hein. It centres on the hospitality shown by the townspeople of Gander, Newfoundland, to the seven thousand travellers forced to land there when American air space was closed following the terrorist attacks on 11 September 2001.

"This Tree": A tree trunk, which symbolized on stage both the Gander landscape and one of the twin towers, came into leaf during the course of the production.

ACKNOWLEDGEMENTS

Earlier versions of these poems, sometimes with different titles, appeared in the *Antigonish Review*, *Canadian Literature*, the *Fiddlehead*, *Grain*, the *Literary Review of Canada*, the *New Quarterly*, the *Windsor Review*, and in the Caitlin Press anthology of tree poems, *Worth More Standing*. I am grateful to the editors for their encouragement.

New Songs for Orpheus is a kind of updating of Ovid, and my epigraphs from him are taken from the Loeb Classical Library's prose translations of *Metamorphoses* by Frank Justus Miller, and of *Heroides* by Grant Showerman. I was initially spurred to respond to Ovid by a comment Don McKay made in *The Shell of the Tortoise* (Gaspereau Press, 2011) – that it was the dynamism of the natural world that animated the lyric in the first place, and to praise Orpheus "is equivalent to a cook taking credit for the sweetness of the plum and the bitterness of the lemon." My collection mostly tries to look and listen to the real creatures into which Ovid's characters transformed, in an effort to strip away some layers of anthropomorphism and appreciate their otherness – before many of them become extinct. This is a concern that I explored recently from a different perspective in *Earth Words: Conversing with Three Sages* (McGill-Queen's University Press, 2021), and it is one that has been enriched by Eva Meijer's books on animal rights, *Animal Languages* (MIT Press, 2016) and *When Animals Speak* (NYU Press, 2019).

My enthusiasm for Ovid, however, goes back much farther. When I was an undergraduate, I was fortunate enough to be taught Classics by the late Professor Vera Lachman, a Holocaust survivor who in the 1930s had founded a school for Jewish children deprived of education by the Nazis. In the 1960s she took our university Latin class outside to the lily pond to read the great authors. We knew them from our texts, but she had memorized them, a precious cargo in dangerous times. It is her voice I hear when I read them, and parts VI and VII of this book attempt to convey some of her faith in the metamorphic power of our fragile loves.

Other voices have helped shape my poems. Early conversations with the late Bruce Nagle opened possibilities for exploring the *Metamorphoses*, and email exchanges with Bert Almon and John Porter suggested further options. My late wife Julie provided invaluable criticism and encouragement during the writing process of most of the poems in this book, and still provides inspiration. Once again, I want to thank the members of the Vic group for their critical attention: this time, Allan Briesmaster, Sue Chenette, Maureen Hynes, Marvyne Jenoff, and K.D. Miller were especially helpful. Finally, my editor Allan Hepburn has shown exemplary patience, kindness, and support while exercising his characteristically meticulous scrutiny. I'm deeply grateful to them all.